First Eucharist

Liturgy of the Eucharist / Liturgy of the word

Dr. Gerard F. Baumbach
Moya Gullage

Rev. Msgr. John F. Barry
Dr. Eleanor Ann Brownell
Helen Hemmer, I.H.M.
Dr. Norman F. Josaitis
Rev. Michael J. Lanning, O.F.M.
Dr. Marie Murphy
Karen Ryan
Joseph F. Sweeney

Official Theological Consultant
Most Rev. Edward K. Braxton, Ph.D., S.T.D.

Pastoral Consultant
Rev. Virgilio P. Elizondo, Ph.D., S.T.D.

Catechetical and Liturgical Consultants
Dr. Gerard F. Baumbach
Dr. Eleanor Ann Brownell

with
Dr. Thomas H. Groome
Boston College

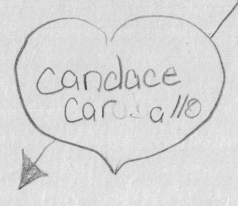

candace
Carosallo

William H. Sadlier, Inc.
9 Pine Street
New York, NY 10005–1002

Nihil Obstat
✠ Most Reverend George O. Wirz
Censor Librorum

Imprimatur
✠ Most Reverend William H. Bullock
Bishop of Madison
July 10, 1995

The *Nihil Obstat* and *Imprimatur* are official declarations that a book or pamphlet is free of doctrinal or moral error. No implication is contained therein that those who have granted the *Nihil Obstat* and *Imprimatur* agree with the contents, opinions, or statements expressed.

Printed in the United States of America.

Home Office:
9 Pine Street
New York, NY 10005–1002

ISBN: 0–8215–2402–X

18 19 20 21 22 23 24/08 07 06 05 04

Acknowledgments
Excerpts and adaptations from *Good News Bible*, copyright © American Bible Society 1966, 1971, 1976, 1979.

Excerpts from the English translation of *The Roman Missal* © 1973, International Committee on English in the Liturgy, Inc. All rights reserved.

"Children of the Lord," © 1976, North American Liturgy Resources (NALR). All rights reserved. "Let There Be Peace on Earth," © 1955, Jan–Lee Music, Honokaa, Hawaii. All rights reserved.

Photo Credits

Jim Saylor — Photo Editor

Mary Kate Coudal — Photo Research

Diane J. Ali: 44.
Gay Bumgamer / Tony Stone Images: 22–23.
Myrleen Cate: 4, 5, 6, 7, 10, 11, 14, 18, 19, 26, 27, 34, 35, 40, 41, 42, 46, 47, 52, 53, 56, 57.
Bernard Hehl / Unicorn: 23 left.
Ken Karp: 12, 15, 20, 22 top, 23 right, 30 left, 31, 45, 48, 49, 54.
NASA: 56–57.
H. Armstrong Roberts, 15 background, 22 left.
The Stock Market / Gary Palaez: 22 bottom; George Disario: 23 center.
Jim Whitmer: 23 bottom, 30 right, 31.

Illustrators
David Barnett: 9, 17, 25, 33, 38–39, 51, 59, 61, 63, 65, 67, 69
Adam Gordon: 58, 60, 64, 68, 70
Olivia McElroy: 4–5, 12, 13, 18, 19, 21, 28, 29, 34, 35, 36, 37, 41, 42, 44, 52–53, 54, 55, 56–57, A
Mike Radencich: 6–7, 14–15, 22–23, 30–31, 38–39, 46–47, 48–49, 75, 77, 78
Bob Shein: 58, 59, 61, 63, 65, 67, 69, 76
Michael Woo: 45, Mass cutout

Contents

A Parish Welcoming Rite

Leader: Join with your friends who are preparing for First Communion. Ask an adult in your family to hold a lighted candle in one hand and place the other hand on your shoulder. Then sing:

Children of the Lord

Carey Landry

♪ We are children of the Lord,
  sons and daughters of Light.
We are children of the Lord,
  and we want to walk in God's Light.

Oh, yes, we are God's children;
  We are the gifts of God's love.
Oh, yes, we are God's children;
  To God alone we belong. ♪

Leader: You are a Catholic. You are a baptized member of the Church, and you have celebrated the sacrament of Reconciliation. Now you will prepare to receive your First Communion.

Read aloud together the special message on your candle.

I,

Candace,

(name)

am preparing to receive Jesus in Holy Communion.

Now say together:

I believe in God our Father, Jesus Christ, the Son of God, and God the Holy Spirit.

I will try to follow Jesus by loving God and others.

I will try not to hurt others.
I will try to be fair to everyone.
I will be a peacemaker.

I will try to live as a good member of the Church.

Please, everyone, help us get ready to receive Jesus in Holy Communion.

(Close by singing "Children of the Lord.")

We Gather Together

Welcome to your First Communion group!

You are very special. You are getting ready to do something wonderful. Soon you will receive Jesus in Holy Communion.

Your families are going to help you to get ready. Your teachers will help you, too. Our whole parish is praying for you.

So many people love and care for you! Most of all, Jesus loves and cares for you. Jesus longs to come to you in Holy Communion. How does that make you feel?

Let's stand in a circle and sing a song about coming together to be with Jesus.

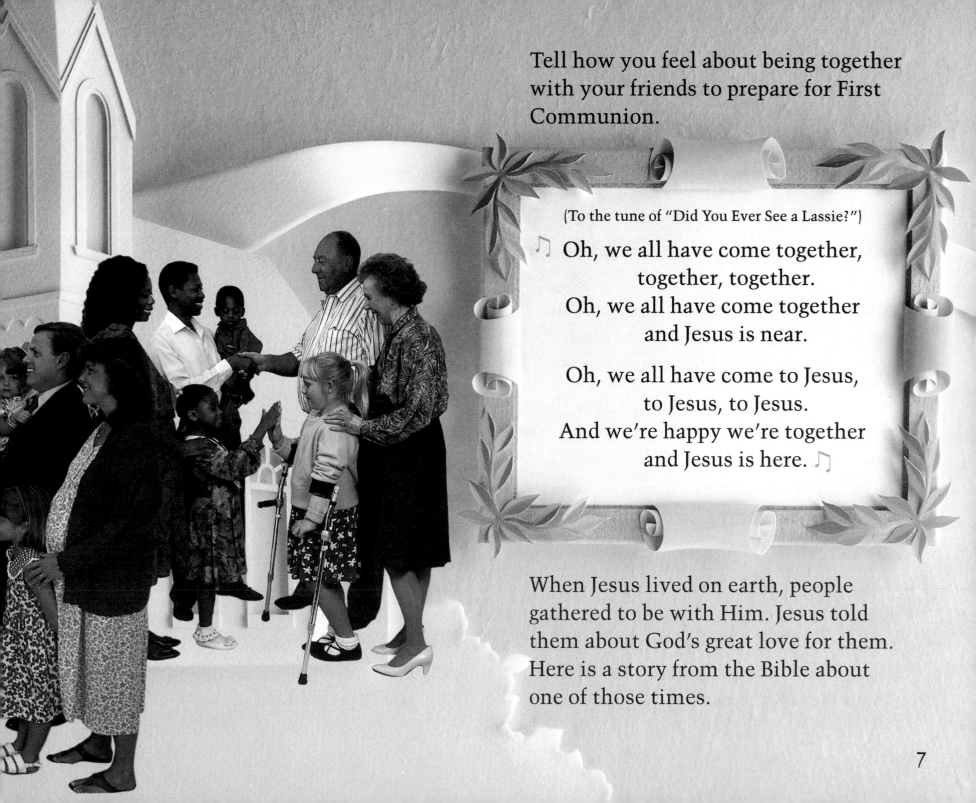

Tell how you feel about being together with your friends to prepare for First Communion.

(To the tune of "Did You Ever See a Lassie?")

♫ Oh, we all have come together,
    together, together.
Oh, we all have come together
    and Jesus is near.

Oh, we all have come to Jesus,
    to Jesus, to Jesus.
And we're happy we're together
    and Jesus is here. ♫

When Jesus lived on earth, people gathered to be with Him. Jesus told them about God's great love for them. Here is a story from the Bible about one of those times.

7

The Loaves and the Fishes

A crowd of five thousand people had been with Jesus all day. They wanted to be near Him and hear His words.

At the end of the day, Jesus knew that the people were very hungry. No one had any food except for a young boy. He had five loaves of bread and two fishes. How could Jesus feed so many people with so little food?

A wonderful thing happened. Jesus took the boy's bread and gave thanks to God. He told His disciples to give the bread to all the people. Then He did the same with the fish.

Everyone had enough to eat. Food was even left over—twelve baskets were full! Jesus had worked a great miracle to feed the hungry people.

Based on John 6:1–4, 8–13

What do you learn from this story about Jesus?

You are gathered together as Jesus' friends to prepare for your First Communion. You will learn how much Jesus cares for you. And soon He will come to you. You will receive Jesus Himself in Holy Communion. He is the Bread of Life.

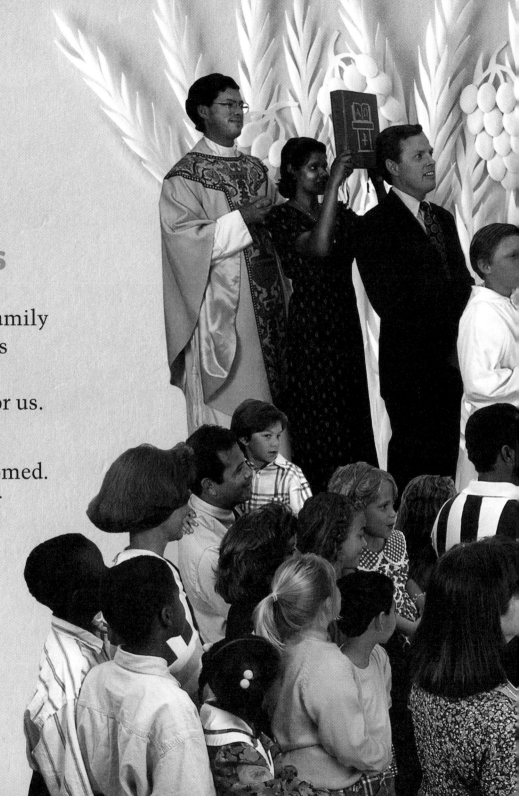

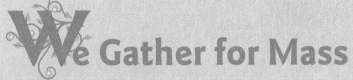e Gather for Mass

Catholics gather together as a parish family
to remember and celebrate that Jesus is
with us. We thank God for Jesus, the
Son of God, and for all that Jesus did for us.
This celebration is called the Mass.

At the beginning of Mass we are welcomed.
We make the sign of the cross together
with the priest. We ask God to have
mercy on us. We praise Him.

Look at the picture.
Tell what is happening.

Now let's read together the prayers
we say at the beginning of Mass.

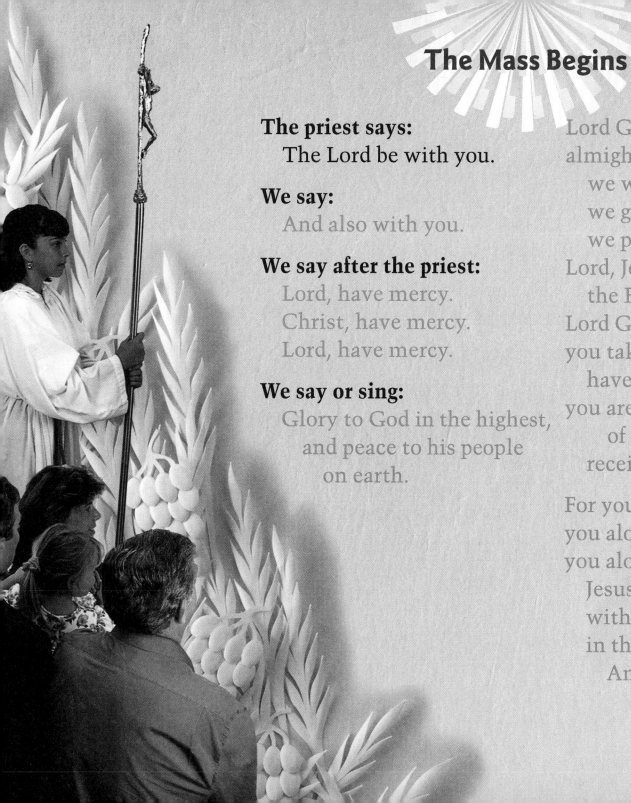

The Mass Begins

The priest says:
  The Lord be with you.

We say:
  And also with you.

We say after the priest:
  Lord, have mercy.
  Christ, have mercy.
  Lord, have mercy.

We say or sing:
  Glory to God in the highest,
    and peace to his people
      on earth.

Lord God, heavenly King,
almighty God and Father,
  we worship you,
  we give you thanks,
  we praise you for your glory.
Lord, Jesus Christ, only Son of
  the Father,
Lord God, Lamb of God,
you take away the sin of the world:
  have mercy on us;
you are seated at the right hand
    of the Father:
  receive our prayer.

For you alone are the Holy One,
you alone are the Lord,
you alone are the Most High,
  Jesus Christ,
  with the Holy Spirit,
  in the glory of God the Father.
    Amen.

11

Jesus Is With Us

We sing and pray together.

We pray the Our Father.

We ask for God's mercy.

We praise God.

Do you remember what happens at the beginning of Mass? Tell about it.

Then color only the signs that tell what we do as Mass begins.

Now gather in a prayer circle. Try to be very still—inside and outside.

Look at the song in the back of your book. Follow the words. Listen to the music. Can you learn the first verse by heart? Sing it together as a closing prayer.

Will you ask your family to take you to Mass this Sunday?

At Home

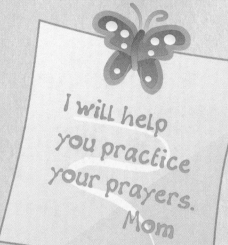

Welcome to your child's First Communion preparation program! We begin as every Mass begins—by extending welcome. We want to be sure that your child truly feels welcome in the First Communion group, as well as in the parish. Lesson One is planned to help your child feel at home and welcome in the parish family. The following steps may help as you go through the lesson with your child.

1. Read through the chapter with your child. Encourage your child to teach you the song he or she learned and to tell you the Bible story of Jesus feeding the hungry people.

2. Help your child understand what happens as the Mass begins. Go over the responses together. Have your child bring this Eucharist book to Mass to follow each part and to make the responses.

3. Review the last page of the lesson which asks your child to remember what happens at the beginning of Mass. Learn and sing the song on the inside back cover of the book.

4. Spend a few minutes doing the **At Home** activity on this page together. You have made an excellent start in working with your parish to prepare your child for this most important step in his or her spiritual life— First Communion.

Make a special family bulletin board.

Invite family members to add notes telling you:

✦ that they are praying for you;

✦ what they will do to help you prepare.

Make a card like this to begin your bulletin board display.

I will help you practice your prayers. Mom

Your special day is coming, and I will pray for you. Uncle Fred

Dear God,

You have called me by my name

Candace Caraballo .

(name)

I am Your child. Help me prepare to receive Jesus, Your Son, in Holy Communion.

We Listen

Let's sit in a listening circle.
Think of sounds that make you happy.
What might they be?

A church bell ringing?
Your mother singing?

The summer wind sighing?
A sea gull crying?

A happy song playing?
Your own voice praying?

Name your favorite sounds.
Tell why you like them.

Sometimes we must listen very hard to hear important things. Sometimes we must listen very hard to hear God speak to us.

We listen to God's word at Mass. How do you try to listen well to God's word?

What might you do to be a better listener?

Listening to God's Word

Here is a song from the Bible.
It is called a psalm.
Jesus often listened to these words
when He was your age.

Listen to the psalm.

Praise the Lord from the heavens,
　praise Him in the heights.
Praise the Lord, sun and moon,
　praise God, you shining stars.

Praise the Lord, great whales,
　praise Him, all fish of the sea.
Praise the Lord, all mountains and hills,
　praise God, all animals, all birds that fly.

Praise the Lord, all people everywhere!
　Praise God always!

Based on Psalm 148: 1, 3, 7, 9, 10, 13

Can you imagine how the sun and
the stars praise God?

Imagine how whales and lions
and eagles praise God!

How can we praise God?
Put yourself in the picture,
praising Him.

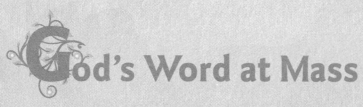

God's Word at Mass

We listen to readings from the Bible at Mass. During the Liturgy of the Word, the word of God is read to us from the Bible. We listen and pray a psalm, too.

Before the gospel is read, we join with our parish family in song. We sing "Alleluia" to say how happy we are to listen to the good news. In the gospel we hear the good news of Jesus Christ, the Son of God.

We listen as the priest or deacon explains what God's word means for us. This is called the homily or sermon. Then all together we proclaim our Catholic faith in the Creed.

During the Prayer of the Faithful we pray for the Church, our leaders, and all people. We pray quietly for our own needs, too.

This ends the Liturgy of the Word, the first part of the Mass.

The Liturgy of the Word

After the first and second reading, the lector says:
The word of the Lord.
We answer:
Thanks be to God.

After the gospel, the deacon or priest says:
The gospel of the Lord.
We answer:
Praise to you, Lord Jesus Christ.

We all stand to make our Profession of Faith. (See the Nicene Creed on page 71.)

After the Creed, we say the Prayer of the Faithful. We usually say after each prayer:
Lord, hear our prayer.

Praying and Listening

What would you like to pray for at the Prayer of the Faithful? Write your prayer here.

For _____

_____

Take turns reading your prayers aloud. After each one, answer together:

"Lord, hear our prayer."

Cut out the heart in the back of the book. Write on it one way you will be a better listener at Mass. Join your heart to all the others on a string.

Now gather in your prayer circle. Hold the string of hearts up high as you sing this listening song.

(To the tune of "Frère Jacques")

♪ We will listen, we will listen
To Your word, to Your word.
Speak and we will hear You,
Jesus, give us all a
Listening heart, listening heart. ♪

Family Focus

After the Introductory Rites at Mass, we begin the part of the Mass called the Liturgy of the Word. The Church teaches us that God is present to us in a unique way in Scripture. The first reading is from the Old Testament (or, in the Easter season, from the Acts of the Apostles in the New Testament). It is followed by the psalm, a response to God's word. The second reading is from the letters of the New Testament. Then we stand for the proclaiming of the gospel, the good news of Jesus Christ. We respond by affirming our belief in the Creed and by asking God's help in the Prayer of the Faithful.

1. The theme of this chapter is listening. Go through the lesson with your child. Read aloud especially the opening poem (page 14) and the psalm (page 16).

2. Help your child understand that sometimes it is hard to listen, especially when the words are too difficult. Encourage your child to listen to the readings at Mass this week. Afterward talk together about what you both heard for your lives in the Liturgy of the Word.

3. Encourage your child to tell you about the promise to listen well at Mass this week. Sing the listening song together on page 20. Then do the **At Home** activity.

At Home

Make a bookmark like the one you see here. Decorate your bookmark. Write these words on it:

Praise
God
Always!

Remember these words and share them with others.
Keep your bookmark in your
First Communion book.

21

3 We Give Gifts

God has given us so many gifts!

Look at these pictures.
They show some of God's gifts
to us. Talk about them together.

What do you think we should say
to God for all these gifts?

One way to say thank You to God is to give a gift in return. Can you think of a gift you can give to God?

We will learn today that we both give and receive gifts at Mass. Let's begin by listening to a story Jesus told about God's gifts.

23

God's Gifts

One day many people had come to listen to Jesus. He saw that some of them were tired and worried about many things. Some of them were ragged and poor.

They needed to hear about God's love and care for them!

Jesus pointed to the birds that were flying around them.

"Look at the birds in the sky," Jesus said. "They don't plant or harvest. Yet your Father in heaven takes care of them. Aren't you worth more than many birds?"

Then He said, "Look how the wild flowers grow. They don't worry about what clothes to wear.

Yet a king is not dressed as beautifully as these flowers are."

Jesus looked at the people with love. He said, "Don't worry about what to eat or what to wear. If God clothes the wild flowers and feeds the birds, how much more must He care for you! You are worth so much more than birds and flowers!"

Based on Matthew 6:25–32

God loves and cares for us, too. God wants us to love and care for one another.

God's love for us is so great that He gave us the gift of Jesus.

We thank God for the gift of Jesus, especially at Mass.

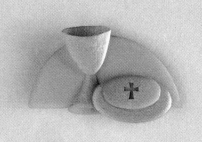

Gifts of Bread and Wine

At Mass we bring gifts of bread and wine to the altar. Our gifts are signs of ourselves. This is our way of saying, "Thank You, God, for all You have given us."

The word *Eucharist* means "giving thanks."

The priest asks God to accept the gifts of bread and wine and the gift of ourselves that we offer.

A sacrifice is an offering to God of something important. A sacrifice is a special gift of love.

Jesus offered the greatest sacrifice of all. He gave His life for us. He died for us on the cross and rose again to be with us always.

At Mass, we remember and celebrate Jesus' life, death, and resurrection. Jesus gives Himself to us in Holy Communion.

Can you learn the responses we make at this part of the Mass?

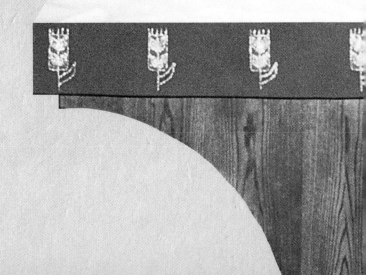

The Preparation of the Gifts

We bring our gifts of bread and wine to the altar.

The priest praises and thanks God for the gift of bread.

We answer:
Blessed be God for ever.

Then the priest thanks God for the gift of wine.

We answer:
Blessed be God for ever.

The priest then prays that we, with our gifts of bread and wine, will be acceptable to God the Father.

We answer:
May the Lord accept the sacrifice at your hands
for the praise and glory of his name,
for our good, and the good of all his Church.

Gifts of Love

What is the greatest gift we receive at Mass?

What do we answer when the priest praises and thanks God for the gifts of bread and wine? Find the answer. Use one color to fill in the spaces with an "X." Then use other colors to complete the stained-glass window.

Pray the prayer together.

Think for a moment. Choose an act of love you will do for someone this week. Offer it to God at Mass this Sunday.

At Home

Every child loves to receive gifts. Perhaps your child has discovered the delight of *giving* gifts as well. Talk with your child about gifts we give to show our love for others. This will also help them come to understand the meaning of sacrifice.

At the beginning of the Liturgy of the Eucharist we present gifts of bread and wine to God. We also give gifts to support our parish and to help the poor. We bring our gifts to the altar as signs of ourselves.

1. Read through the chapter together. Talk about the different kinds of gifts we receive and give. Then invite your child to tell you the Bible story.

2. Ask your child to tell you what a *sacrifice* is. Ask what great sacrifice Jesus made for us. Help your child to understand that we, too, can offer ourselves to God in little ways every day.

3. Go over the responses we make during the Preparation of the Gifts at Mass.

4. Ask your child to share with you the activity on page 28. Pray the prayer together. Then do the **At Home** activity.

Invite everyone in the family to show love and care for others by making little gifts for them this week.

Trace and cut out a cloud and rainbow. On the cloud write: **Our Gifts to God**.

Go to the store for Mrs. Schork

WASH CAR FOR JIM

Help Mom with laundry

Send cheerful note to Grandpa

Our Gifts to God

For each color in the rainbow, have the members of your family write one way they will help others. Hang your finished rainbow in a place where everyone will see it and remember the promises that were made.

4 We Remember

Think for a minute.
Are you a good "remember-er"?
When people you love are far away,
how do you remember them?

Look at the pictures. Pick some
ways you remember people. Talk
about them with your friends.

If you wanted someone to
remember you always, what
would you do?

Jesus wants us to remember Him
always. So He did something
wonderful. What do you think
He did?

Do This in Memory of Me

Jesus wants us to remember Him always. He wants us to remember His love for us. He wants us to remember especially what He did for us when He died on the cross.

This is what Jesus did on the night before He died for us.

Based on Luke 22:19–20

The Last Supper

Jesus gathered His friends around Him for a special meal.

Jesus took bread and gave thanks to God. He then broke the bread and gave it to His friends, saying, "Take this, all of you, and eat it: this is My Body which will be given up for you."

When the meal was over, Jesus took a cup of wine. He gave thanks to God and handed the cup to each of His friends, saying, "Take this, all of you, and drink from it: this is the cup of my blood, the blood of the new and everlasting covenant. It will be shed for you and for all so that sins may be forgiven. Do this in memory of Me."

At every Mass we remember the Last Supper and the gift of Himself that Jesus gave to us.
We also remember and enter into His death and resurrection.
We thank God that Jesus is with us always in the Eucharist.

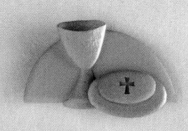

We Pray the Eucharistic Prayer

At Mass Jesus once again does for us what He did at the Last Supper. He does this through the words and actions of the priest who offers our gifts of bread and wine to God. The priest says and does what Jesus did at the Last Supper.

By the power of the Holy Spirit and the words and actions of the priest, the bread and wine become Jesus Himself. This is called the consecration of the Mass. What looks like bread and tastes like bread is not bread anymore. What looks like wine and tastes like wine is not wine anymore.

The bread and wine have become the Body and Blood of Christ.

We proclaim our faith, singing:
Christ has died,
Christ is risen,
Christ will come again.

We give thanks to God for the gift of Jesus in the Eucharist. Remember, the word *Eucharist* means "giving thanks." We say or sing "Amen!" This means "yes, I believe." We believe Jesus is really present in the Eucharist.

This is how we can join in the eucharistic prayer.

The Eucharistic Prayer

Priest: The Lord be with you.
All: And also with you.

Priest: Lift up your hearts.
All: We lift them up to the Lord.

Priest: Let us give thanks to the Lord our God.
All: It is right to give him thanks and praise.

We pray with the priest:
Holy, holy, holy Lord, God of power and might,
heaven and earth are full of your glory.
Hosanna in the highest.
Blessed is he who comes in the name of the Lord.
Hosanna in the highest.

We proclaim our faith:
Christ has died,
Christ is risen,
Christ will come again.

Priest:
Through him,
with him,
in him,
in the unity of the Holy Spirit,
all glory and honor is yours,
almighty Father,
for ever and ever.

All: Amen.

35

We Remember

Tell a partner the story of the Last Supper.

Here is a song about the Last Supper. Listen to it, then sing it together.

Do This in Remembrance of Me

Lou Fortunate

♪ Lord, we gather 'round your table
First to hear Your holy word;
Then partake with one another of the
    eucharistic food.
"Do this in remembrance of Me."
"Do this in remembrance of Me."

Jesus told the twelve apostles, "I will
    give you living bread.
Take and eat; this is My Body."
Then He turned to them and said:
"Do this in remembrance of Me."
"Do this in remembrance of Me." ♪

Now decorate and pray this prayer.

JESUS

I, _____ ,
(name)

thank You for being with us at Mass. Help me to love others as You did.

Family Focus

Begin this important lesson by remembering with your child the ways members of your family take care of one another. Mention something special your child has done this week to help someone.

The Second Vatican Council reminds us that the Eucharist is "the source and the summit of our faith." There is nothing more important that we do together as a Catholic community. The celebration of the Eucharist is our greatest prayer of thanksgiving to God. In this celebration we do what Jesus has asked us to do: we remember and enter into His saving death and resurrection. Through the Eucharist we share in the one sacrifice of Christ.

Your reverence for the Eucharist and your faithful participation at Mass each week will be a powerful example for your child's growing appreciation and living of the Eucharist.

1. Read through the lesson together. Allow your child time to talk about gifts. Then read the gospel account of the Last Supper.

2. Help your child understand that when we receive Jesus in Holy Communion our "Amen" means we believe that Jesus is really present.

3. Do the **At Home** activity together.

At Home

Make placecards for a special family meal. There should be one card for each member of the family. You might like to write a special message for each family member inside the cards.

Before sharing the meal, invite the family to join you in a grace prayer.

† **Dear God,**
   Bless this food we share.
   Thank You for all Your gifts. Amen.

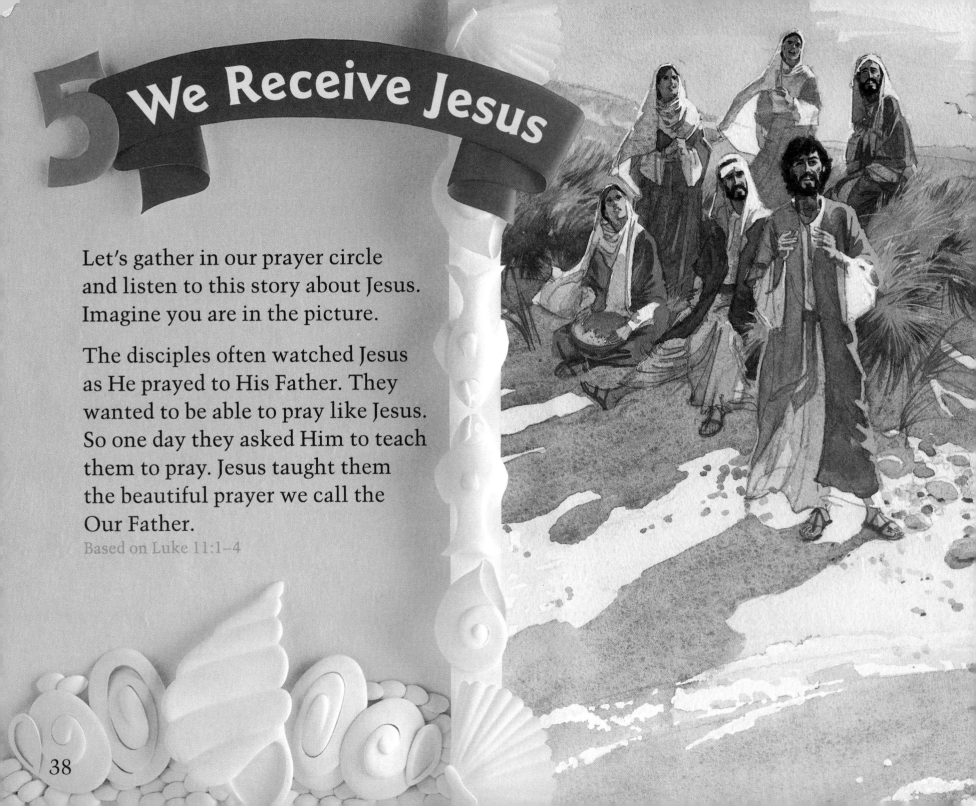

5 We Receive Jesus

Let's gather in our prayer circle and listen to this story about Jesus. Imagine you are in the picture.

The disciples often watched Jesus as He prayed to His Father. They wanted to be able to pray like Jesus. So one day they asked Him to teach them to pray. Jesus taught them the beautiful prayer we call the Our Father.

Based on Luke 11:1–4

When we pray the Our Father,
we say,

Our Father, who art in heaven,
hallowed be thy name;
thy kingdom come;
thy will be done on earth
as it is in heaven.
Give us this day our daily bread;
and forgive us our trespasses
as we forgive those
who trespass against us;
and lead us not into temptation,
but deliver us from evil.

This prayer is called the Our Father.
Sometimes it is called the Lord's
Prayer because Jesus gave it to us.

Now let's pray together the prayer
that Jesus taught us.

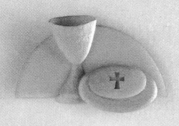

The Communion of the Mass

We pray the Our Father to begin the Communion time of the Mass.

Before we receive Jesus in Holy Communion, we ask God to forgive us as we forgive others.

We prepare to receive Jesus when we try to be forgiving and peaceful people.

To remind us of this, we turn to those around us and give them a sign of Christ's own peace. This shows that we really will try to be peacemakers like Jesus.

The priest takes the host and breaks it. He does this to show that all of us share in the one Bread of Life when we receive Jesus in Holy Communion.

We pray together to Jesus, the Lamb of God, asking Him to forgive our sins and to give us peace.

Then the priest holds up the host.
We pray together:
"Lord, I am not worthy to receive you,
    but only say the word and I shall
        be healed."

Preparing for Communion

To show respect and love for Jesus, Catholics fast before receiving Holy Communion. This means that we do not eat or drink anything for one hour before Communion time. However, we can take water and medicine.

Jesus Comes to Us

We are now ready to receive Jesus in Holy Communion. The priest or eucharistic minister places the Host in our hand or on our tongue, saying, "The body of Christ." We answer "Amen."

Remember, the word *Amen* means "yes, I believe." We believe that Jesus is really present in the Eucharist.

If we are to receive from the cup, the minister says, "The blood of Christ." Again we answer "Amen."

After receiving Jesus, we sing a thanksgiving song together. Then we spend quiet time talking to Jesus. We thank Him for coming to us. We ask Him to help us to live as His friends. We ask Jesus to take care of our families, our friends, and everyone in need.

The Communion of the Mass

Together with the priest we pray the Our Father. Then the priest says,

Priest: Deliver us, Lord, from every evil, and grant us peace in our day. In your mercy keep us free from sin and protect us from all anxiety as we wait in joyful hope for the coming of our Savior, Jesus Christ.

All: For the kingdom, the power and the glory are yours, now and for ever.

Priest: The peace of the Lord be with you always.

All: And also with you.

We give a sign of Christ's peace to those around us.

All: Lamb of God, you take away the sins of the world: have mercy on us. (2 times) Lamb of God, you take away the sins of the world: grant us peace.

All: Lord, I am not worthy to receive you, but only say the word and I shall be healed.

Now we are ready to receive Jesus in Holy Communion.

Priest or minister: The body of Christ.

We answer: Amen.

Priest or minister: The blood of Christ.

We answer: Amen.

Jesus is Really Present

Explain why you answer "Amen" when you receive Jesus in Holy Communion.

What will you say to Jesus when you receive Him in Holy Communion?

Learn "My Communion Prayer" song by heart. Then sign your name to help you remember to pray it when you receive Jesus.

Now let's sing the prayer song together.

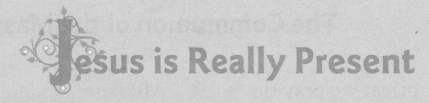

My Communion Prayer

Jesus, You come to me
As Bread to feed me,
Friend to heal me,
Light to lead me.
Welcome, Jesus, welcome.

_____
(name)

Family Focus

At Home

Soon your child will be receiving Jesus in Holy Communion. Try to create among *all* the family members an atmosphere of prayerful anticipation. Gently lead your child to think more about the joy of receiving Jesus, rather than the gifts he or she is expecting to receive.

1. Ask your child to tell you the way Jesus taught His disciples to pray. Point out that we pray the Our Father before receiving Jesus in Holy Communion. Have your child tell you what it means to say "forgive us our trespasses as we forgive those who trespass against us."

2. Talk about the sign of peace we share before receiving Jesus. How can we be people who give peace? Then go over the responses that we make at the Communion of the Mass.

3. Practice with your child how to receive the Host. Do it gently, calmly so that your child will not be nervous. If your child is to receive from the cup, practice that also.

4. Help your child to think about what he or she will do after receiving Jesus. Ask, "What will you say to Him? For whom will you pray?" Say (or sing) *My First Communion Song* on the inside back cover. Then do the **At Home** activity together.

Make a First Communion memory box. Use a shoe box (or a box of a similar size). Decorate the outside with drawings. Write "My First Communion Memories" on the cover.

Make a list of what you will put in your box. You might like to write a letter or make a tape telling about your First Communion Day.

photographs   _____   _____

prayer card   _____   _____

45

How to Receive Communion

This is how we receive the Body of Christ.

✦ Prepare your heart to welcome Jesus.

✦ Walk to the altar with hands joined.

✦ You can choose to receive the Host in your hand. As your turn comes, cup your left hand on top of your right hand (or the opposite if you are left-handed).

✦ When you hear the words "The body of Christ," answer "Amen."

✦ After the Host is placed in your hand, carefully place it in your mouth. Then return to your seat.

✦ You can choose to receive the Host on your tongue. After you answer "Amen," hold your head up and gently put out your tongue. After the Host is placed on your tongue, return to your seat. Swallow the Host.

This is how we receive the Blood of Christ.

✤ If you are to receive from the cup, swallow the Host and move to the minister holding the cup.

✤ When you hear the words "The blood of Christ," answer "Amen."

✤ Then take a sip from the cup.

✤ Return to your seat.

After Receiving Communion

✤ Sing the Communion song with your parish family.

✤ Spend time just with Jesus. Tell Him the things for which you want to thank Him. Then talk to Him about whatever is in your heart. Ask Him to help you live as His friend.

6 Jesus Is With Us Always

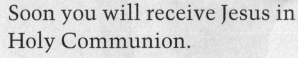

Soon you will receive Jesus in Holy Communion.
What a happy day that will be!
Happiness is something that we need to share.
How can you share your happiness that Jesus is coming to you?

What can you do for. . .
- ✦ your family?
- ✦ someone who is sick?
- ✦ someone who is sad?
- ✦ someone who is in need?

The Church teaches us that Catholics must receive Holy Communion at least once a year. But we should try to receive Jesus every time we go to Mass. How wonderful it is that we can do this!

Let's gather in a prayer circle. Take turns coming to the center. Say, "I can share my happiness by

_____."

Look at "My First Communion Song" on the inside back cover of your book.

Sing verses two and three together, asking Jesus to help us love and serve others.

49

You Are Light

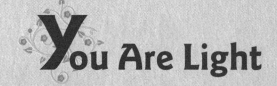

One day Jesus said to His disciples,

"You are the light of the world.
People do not light a lamp
and then put it under a basket.
No, they put it on a table
so that everyone in the house can see.
You must let your light
shine before everyone
so that all will see
the light within you
and the good that you do.
Then they will praise God in heaven."

Based on Matthew 5:14–16

Jesus wants us to be like shining lights.

We are lights when we . . .
- ✤ do and say good things,
- ✤ show kindness to people,
- ✤ love God and others as Jesus did,
- ✤ are fair and help to make peace.

Everyone who sees us will know that God is with us. They will be happy and praise God.

In Holy Communion Jesus helps us to be like a light that shows God's love.

When you receive Jesus, ask Him to be with you always so that you can show God's love to everyone.

We Go in Peace

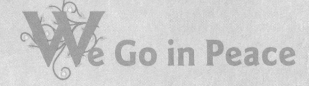

As Mass ends, the priest blesses us. We make the sign of the cross and answer "Amen."

The sign of the cross reminds us that through Baptism we are members of God's Church and are disciples of Jesus Christ. As His friends, we carry on Jesus' work of love and service.

Then we are sent forth to live the Eucharist we have celebrated. The priest or deacon says, "Go in peace to love and serve the Lord."

We answer, "Thanks be to God."

Now we are to go forth and live the Mass by loving and helping others.

The Mass Ends

The priest prays:
The Lord be with you.

We answer:
And also with you.

The priest prays:
May almighty God bless you,
the Father, and the Son, †
and the Holy Spirit.

We answer:
Amen.

**The priest or deacon says one of
the following:**

✤ Go in peace to love and serve the Lord.

✤ Go in the peace of Christ.

✤ The Mass is ended, go in peace.

We answer:
Thanks be to God.

We sing together a closing hymn.

53

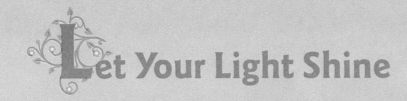

Let Your Light Shine

As a reminder to go in peace to love and serve others, cut out the lantern in the back of your book. Write your name on it. Decide and share how you will try to be a "light" to others this week.

Now gather again in your prayer circle. Hold your lanterns up and pray together:

† Jesus, help us to let Your light shine in us by being people who love and serve.

With your friends, hang your lantern on the bulletin board. When you see the lanterns, remember to let your light shine for others.

Now take your neighbors' hands and pray the Our Father together to end our last lesson.

At Home

Your child is now ready to receive Jesus in Holy Communion. You and your child have come a long way during this preparation time. You have entered into the meaning of the Mass and prepared your own heart, as well as your child's, for this beautiful moment in your child's life.

1. Go through the chapter together. Talk to your child about what it means to be a "light." Light a lamp in a dark room, then cover it with a box. Ask your child, "What good is the lamp now?" Help your First Communicant to see that Jesus wants us to *show* Him to others through what we do and what we say. That is why, at the end of Mass, we are told to "go in peace to love and serve the Lord."

2. Go over the responses for the Concluding Rite of the Mass. Have your child tell you how he or she will try to be a "light" by loving and serving others. Then do the **At Home** activity together.

3. Help your child cut out the cross from the back of the book. Put yarn through the top so it will go around your child's neck. Have your child write his or her name on it. Bring it to the **Sending Forth Rite** (pages 56–57).

Make a "Sundays with Jesus" mobile. This will help you to remember all that you have learned as you prepare to receive your First Communion.

Use a clothes hanger as the base. Cut out a large sun and print the words "Sundays with Jesus." Then draw and cut out other symbols to help you remember Jesus' gift of Himself to us. Add your own ideas.

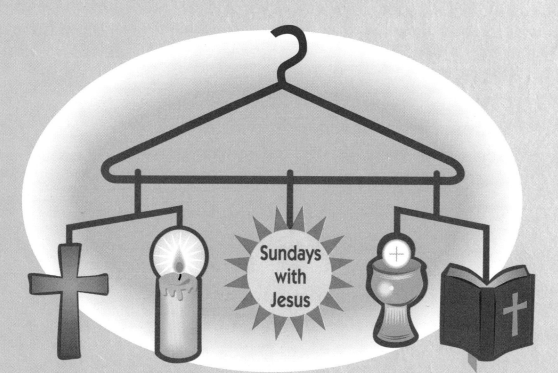

Sundays with Jesus

A Sending Forth Rite

Hold your cross and walk to the altar with your parent or guardian.

Leader: Dear children, you have received our Lord Jesus Christ in Holy Communion. May He be with you always.

All: And also with you.

Leader: Remember always that you belong to Jesus Christ. You are baptized in His name. You have now received His Body and Blood to nourish and strengthen you to live as His friends. This means that in Holy Communion Jesus forgives your venial sins and helps you to keep away from mortal sin. As a reminder of your life in Jesus Christ, your parent or guardian will place the cross around your neck.

Parent (Places the cross around the child's neck, saying)**:**

_____(Name)_____, I place this cross around your neck as a reminder that Jesus, whom you have received in the Eucharist, will be with you always. He will help you to live as His friend.

Children: Amen. Jesus, we promise to come to You often in Holy Communion.

Leader: The whole Church, especially our own parish, rejoices with you. As I call your name, come and receive your certificate of First Communion.

Leader: Remember, Jesus will be with you as you go forth to love and serve others in His name. Now let us all go in peace as we sing.

Let There Be Peace on Earth

Sy Miller and Jill Jackson

♫ Let there be peace on earth
and let it begin with me;
Let there be peace on earth,
The peace that was meant to be.

With God as our Father,
We are family.
Let us walk now together
 in perfect harmony.

Let peace begin with me,
Let this be the moment now.
With ev'ry step I take,
Let this be my solemn vow.
To take each moment
 and live each moment
 in peace eternally.

Let there be peace on earth
 and let it begin with me. ♫

57

Summary: I Will Remember

1 **What does the word Eucharist mean?**

Eucharist means "giving thanks." In the Eucharist we give thanks to God.

2 **Why do we give thanks to God?**

We give thanks to God for Jesus, God's greatest gift to us.

3 **What did Jesus do for us?**

Jesus showed us how to live our faith. He died on the cross for us and rose again that we might have a new life.

4 **When did Jesus give us the Eucharist?**

Jesus gave us the Eucharist at the Last Supper, the night before He died.

5 **What happens to the bread and wine at Mass?**

By the power of the Holy Spirit and the words and actions of the priest, the bread and wine become the Body and Blood of Christ.

6 **Whom do we receive in Holy Communion?**

We receive Jesus, the Bread of Life.

Jesus,
thank You
for being
our
Bread of Life.

Preparing for Jesus

1

I am preparing to receive Holy Communion

1. I am getting ready to receive Jesus in

Holy _____ .

2. Jesus feeds us with Himself. He is our

_____ of _____ .

3. We gather to celebrate as Jesus' family

at _____ .

I remember God's word

Unscramble the words to complete the Bible story. Write the words in the bread.

rhyung   kashnt   hfsi   oyb

sJsue   darbe

A crowd of people gathered to listen to

_____ . They stayed with Him

all day. There was very little food. Jesus

knew they must be very _____ .

A young _____ had some food.

Jesus gave _____ to God

for the food. Jesus fed the crowd with

five loaves of _____ and

two _____ .

Jesus, help me to have a listening heart. Amen.

Preparing for Jesus

2

I am preparing to receive Holy Communion

1. We listen to God's stories from the

_____ .

2. At Mass we listen to God's stories in

the Liturgy of the _____ .

3. At Mass we stand to hear the
good news of Jesus in the

_____ .

I remember God's word

Choose your favorite lines from Psalm 148 on page 16. The picture on the cover of the booklet will remind you of the psalm. Then draw and color a picture of your choice.

_____

_____

_____

_____

fold

Here is a
poem to learn.

If God clothes flowers
Feeds birds of air,
Then how much more
God's loving care
For us who are
His children!

Preparing for Jesus

3

I am preparing to receive Holy Communion

1. We bring to the altar gifts of

_____ and _____ .

2. The priest offers our gifts to

_____ .

3. We pray together,

"Blessed be God _____ ."

I remember God's word

Write the missing words in the puzzle.

1. Look at the _____ in the sky.

2. Your _____ takes care of them.

3. Look how the _____ grow.

4. How much more must God _____ for you.

We thank you, God our Father,

You made us to live for you

and for each other.

We can see and speak

to one another,

and become friends,

and share our joys and sorrows.

And so, Father, we gladly

thank you . . . saying,

"Holy, holy, holy Lord,

God of power and might. . . ."

Preparing for Jesus

4

I am preparing to receive Holy Communion

1. Jesus gave us the gift of Himself at

   the _____ _____ .

2. Jesus is really present in the

   _____ .

3. Jesus wants us to remember that He is

   with us _____ .

fold

I remember God's word

Use the code.
What words did Jesus say at the
Last Supper?

A D E F H I M N O R S T Y

When do we do what Jesus asked us to do?

Our Father . . .
Give us this day
our daily bread.
Give us Your Son,
Jesus,
our Bread of Life.

Preparing for Jesus

5

I am preparing to receive Holy Communion

1. Before Communion we give one another a sign of Christ's

_____ .

2. When the priest or minister says, "The body of Christ," we answer,

"_____ ."

3. What will you do after receiving Jesus?

_____

_____

I remember God's word

The disciples said, "Lord, teach us to pray."

What prayer did Jesus teach them?

Using yellow, start to color at the →. Then color every other letter.

Now write the name of the prayer inside the window. Decorate.

Pray this prayer with someone in your family.
Pray it with your parish community at Mass this week.

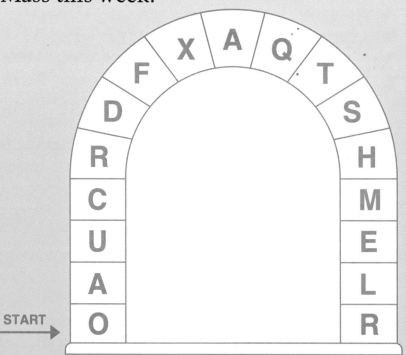

For family, friends, and
   all we love,
Thank You, God!

For the world You give us
   to take care of,
Thank You, God!

For the gift of Jesus,
our Bread of Life,
Thank You, God!

   Amen.

Preparing for Jesus

6

I am preparing to receive Holy Communion

1. When the priest blesses us we make

the _____ of the _____ .

2. At the end of Mass we are told, "Go in

peace to love and _____

the _____ ."

3. We answer,

"_____ be to _____ ."

fold

I remember God's word

How are you a "light"? What did Jesus tell you to do with your light?

_____

_____

How will you let your light shine this week?

I will . . .

☐ be helpful at home

☐ be kind to someone I don't like

☐ pray for someone who is sad or sick

☐ play fair

☐ _____

_____

Nicene Creed

e believe in one God,
the Father, the Almighty,
maker of heaven and earth,
of all that is seen and unseen.

We believe in one Lord, Jesus Christ,
the only Son of God,
eternally begotten of the Father,
God from God, Light from Light,
true God from true God,
begotten, not made, one in Being
    with the Father.
Through him all things were made.
For us men and for our salvation
    he came down from heaven:

by the power of the Holy Spirit
he was born of the Virgin Mary,
    and became man.

For our sake he was crucified under
    Pontius Pilate;
he suffered, died, and was buried.

On the third day he rose again
    in fulfillment of the Scriptures;
he ascended into heaven
    and is seated at the right hand
    of the Father.
He will come again in glory to judge
    the living and the dead,
    and his kingdom will have no end.
We believe in the Holy Spirit, the Lord,
    the giver of life,
who proceeds from the Father and
    the Son.
With the Father and the Son he is
    worshiped and glorified.
He has spoken through the Prophets.
We believe in one holy catholic and
    apostolic Church.
We acknowledge one baptism for the
    forgiveness of sins.
We look for the resurrection of the
    dead,
    and the life of the world to come.
        Amen.

Apostles' Creed

believe in God, the Father almighty,
   creator of heaven and earth.

I believe in Jesus Christ, his only Son, our Lord.
   He was conceived by the power of the Holy Spirit
      and born of the Virgin Mary.
He suffered under Pontius Pilate,
   was crucified, died, and was buried.
He descended to the dead.
On the third day he rose again.
He ascended into heaven,
   and is seated at the right hand of the Father.
He will come again to judge the living and the dead.

I believe in the Holy Spirit,
   the holy catholic Church,
   the communion of saints,
   the forgiveness of sins,
   the resurrection of the body,
   and the life everlasting. Amen.

PRAYERS

Prayer Before Communion

esus, You are my Bread of Life. Help me to welcome You into my heart. Thank You for sharing God's life with me. Help me to be true to You always.

Prayer After Communion

esus, thank You for coming to me in Holy Communion. You come to live within me. You fill me with Your life. I love You very much. Help me to grow in loving You. Help me to be and do all that You wish. Help me to live Your way of love.

Prayer of Quiet

Sit in a comfortable position. Relax by breathing in and out. Shut out all sights and sounds. Each time you breathe in and out, say the name

Glory to the Father

lory to the Father, and to the Son, and to the Holy Spirit: as it was in the beginning, is now, and will be for ever. Amen.

Grace Before Meals

Bless us, O Lord,
and these Your gifts
that we are about to receive
from Your bounty,
through Christ our Lord. Amen.

Grace After Meals

We give You thanks,
almighty God,
for these and all Your gifts
that we have received through
Christ our Lord. Amen.

Morning Offering

My God, I offer You today
All that I think and do and say,
Uniting it with what was done
On earth, by Jesus Christ, Your Son.

Evening Prayer

Dear God, before I sleep I want
to thank You for this day so
full of Your kindness and
Your joy. I close my eyes to rest safe
in Your loving care.

Come
Celebrate
With Me

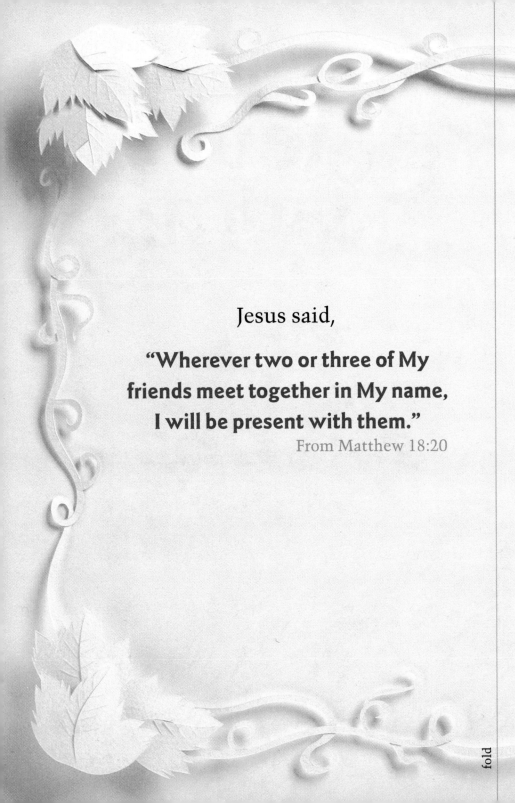

Jesus said,

"Wherever two or three of My friends meet together in My name, I will be present with them."

From Matthew 18:20

You are invited to join me as I make my First Communion.

_____

(Date)

_____

(Parish)

_____

(Time)

I hope you can come and celebrate my special day!

_____

(First Communicant)

fold

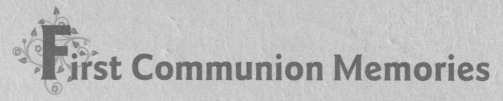First Communion Memories

What a special day!
I will always remember

_____

when I made my First Communion.

Father _____

celebrated with us.

My favorite song was

_____ .

When I received Jesus

in Holy Communion, I said,

"_____,"

yes, I believe.

my photo

I was so happy that my family and friends came to celebrate with me:

_____

_____

_____

_____

_____

my
family

What I will always remember about this day is

_____

_____

_____

_____

Certificate of First Communion

The parish of _____

joyfully celebrates

with _____

who for the first time received

the Eucharist,

the Body and Blood of Jesus Christ,

on _____ in _____
(Date)   (City, State)

Pastor _____